Renoir: *Portrait of Monet*, 1872. Musée Marmottan, Paris

Opposite: Manet: *The Monet Family in their Garden at Argenteuil*, 1874. The Metropolitan Museum of Art, New York

By Nicholas Reed

Published to mark the centenary of Monet's final visits to London in 1899-1901 and including his paintings of

Westminster
Waterloo Bridge
Charing Cross Bridge
The Pool of London
Hyde Park
Green Park

with comparative modern views of the same scenes.

Published by
Lilburne Press
1 Dover House
Maple Road
London
SE20 8EN
Telephone: 0181-659 5776

First edition published
December 1998
© Nicholas Reed 1998
All rights Reserved
ISBN 1 901 167 06 2

Who was Monet?

Claude Monet is probably the best known of the French Impressionist painters. He was born on 14th November 1840 in Paris, but his parents moved shortly afterwards to Le Havre, on the coast of Normandy, where his father set up a ship chandlery business. At school, Monet was constantly drawing caricatures of the teachers. He moved on to sketches of local worthies, and found that he could sell them for a few francs each. When a local shopkeeper displayed them in his window, they were seen by Eugène Boudin, who painted seascapes along the shore, and who persuaded Monet to accompany him on his painting trips. Monet was sceptical to start with, but, as he put it later, "The fact that I've become a painter I owe to Boudin. In his infinite kindness, Boudin instructed me. My eyes were slowly opened and I finally understood nature. I learned at the same time to love it. Six months later, I announced to my father that I wanted to become a painter, and went off to Paris to study art."

Soon after his arrival in 1858, he met Camille Pissarro at the private art academy they both attended. When they moved to a second academy they also met Sisley and Renoir. It was really these four who formed the first Impressionist group, though they would not acquire that name until some fifteen years later, in 1874.

For a time, they all tried to exhibit at the official French Academy, but as their distinctive "impressionist" style became more pronounced, the traditionalist Academy juries continually rejected their works. This led to them putting on their own independent show in 1874, which launched their careers, first, through the scandal the show provoked, and later, as their paintings became increasingly popular with the public.

During the 1860's, however, Monet was frequently in debt, and this cannot have been helped by his living with a woman, Camille Doncieux, who produced a son, Jean, in 1867. His relations then cut off his allowance, and the family had to survive on 'loans' from his artist friends.

Connections with England

In later life, Claude Monet was a considerable Anglophile. His recipe books were full of English dishes, including Welsh rarebit and Yorkshire pudding. He was also a devotee of a "full English" breakfast, and said of the yellow fabric decorating his walls, "It is made in England: my wife gets it from Liberty's."

Camille Pissarro, the "father of French Impressionism", born nine years earlier, also had English connections, and visited the country four times. In fact, his brother and a cousin were already living in England.

Both these painters came to England in 1870. What brought them here?

The German Occupation

In 1870 the Prussians invaded France. To them, any artistic type was regarded with suspicion: artists were probably left-wing, irreligious, and thus a threat to German Order.

In June 1870 Claude Monet married Camille Doncieux, and they went to Trouville for their honeymoon. Soon after, probably in September, Monet got wind of the German invasion, and probably left France hurriedly in order to avoid the call-up to fight in the French forces. He entrusted his wife and child to the care of Mrs Boudin, but they joined him in England soon after.

Their first address was 11 Arundel Street, a street which no longer exists, but was very close to Piccadilly Circus, just off Shaftesbury Avenue. Shortly after, they moved to 1 Bath Place, Kensington. This too has gone, but stood on the site of no 183 Kensington High Street.

The census of April 1871 tells us more. Their landlady at this address was Phoebe Theobald, a widow aged 61, who described herself as a dressmaker, but must have been keeping boarders to earn some extra money. Both Camille, Monet's wife, and their three-year-old son Jean appear in the census, though Claude is absent, and was presumably elsewhere that evening.

It was probably while staying in Kensington that Monet painted "The Thames below Westminster".

The Thames below Westminster, seen from the Embankment, 1994

Monet: *The Thames below Westminster*, 1871.

The Thames below Westminster

The best known Monet picture from this early period is this view, now in the National Gallery in London.

In some ways this painting epitomizes the radicalism of the Impressionists. Establishment artists would have painted castles or other monuments centuries old. Monet's picture shows on the left Westminster Bridge, completed just ten years earlier. On the right is the Victoria Embankment, which was being completed as he painted it: the picture shows a wooden jetty used for the construction being dismantled, with some of the beams floating in the water. Big Ben, behind it, completed in 1858, is exaggerated to dominate the picture, and the Houses of Parliament behind are the buildings finished in 1847, after the disastrous fire of 1834. So everything in the painting is less than thirty years old.

Even at this early period, Monet was interested in misty views: something which was to become very prominent later in his painting, and which can also be seen in his two paintings of the Pool of London.

E W Haslehust: *The Thames at Westminster*, c. 1910. (see page 34)

6

Monet's early paintings of London

Considering that Monet and his family stayed here for at least 6 months: probably from October 1870 to May 1871, he produced remarkably few paintings: only about one a month overall. This may have been the result of depression.

Another French painter, Charles Daubigny, was also in England seeking refuge from the Prussian invasion. That October, while living in Kensington, he stopped writing a letter to light a candle, saying "It's eleven o'clock in the morning. So much for the climate. Fog! Visibility less than two paces." Soon after that, he encountered Monet when they were both working on paintings down by the riverside – probably when Monet was painting the Pool of London. Monet was feeling depressed – among other things, he knew no English, so felt very cut off from the people around him. However, Daubigny offered to introduce him to the French dealer, Durand-Ruel, who had already become the major dealer in French Impressionism. Durand-Ruel had rescued most of his stock from Paris and was preparing to put on a display of French painting in London, at a gallery at 168 New Bond Street. He agreed to display one of Monet's paintings – a view of Trouville – in his December show.

Camille Pissarro had approached the dealer independently, and in January Durand-Ruel wrote to tell Pissarro, much to his surprise, that his friend Monet was in England as well, and gave him Monet's address. The two artists met shortly afterwards.

Pissarro summarised in a letter what he and Monet painted during the spring of 1871.

"Monet and I were very enthusiastic over the London landscapes. Monet worked in the parks, while I, living at Lower Norwood, studied the effects of fog, snow and springtime. We worked from nature, and later on Monet painted in London some superb studies of mist. We also visited the museums. The watercolours and paintings of Turner and Constable certainly had an influence upon us. We admired Gainsborough, Lawrence etc., but we were struck chiefly by the landscape painters."

The Pool of London and the Custom House, 1994

Monet: *The Pool of London*, 1871.

National Museum of Wales, Cardiff

The Pool of London

Monet produced two pictures of the Pool of London, both looking upriver from a pier not far from the Tower of London. One, now in the National Museum of Wales in Cardiff, is only slightly misty, so that many buildings can be identified.

Common to both paintings is London Bridge visible in the distance. This replaced the famous medieval bridge, which had houses on both sides. The bridge that Monet depicts was the one with five stone arches, designed by Sir John Rennie and opened in 1831. It lasted until the 1970's, when it was replaced by the present London Bridge, with three arches. This has far more room for pedestrians, since so many commuters arrive at London Bridge Station and then walk across the Bridge to work in the City. The 1831 bridge was transported to Lake Havasu, Arizona, where it was re-erected, but with one arch less, so that that arch could be used to produce souvenirs of "old London Bridge"!

In Monet's painting the large white and blue building seen on the right is the Custom House, built in 1825. But this is not the original one: in fact it is the sixth on or near this site. The first was built in 1275; when the third one burnt down in the Great Fire of London in 1666, Christopher Wren designed the fourth, but this was accidentally blown up fifty years later.

The spire in the distance is that of the Church of St. Magnus the Martyr. This is one of the many churches which were burnt in 1666, and were rebuilt by Wren.

The much lower tower with a cone on its top is part of Billingsgate Fish Market. The market itself moved to the Isle of Dogs, opposite Greenwich, in 1982. But the building we see now is not what Monet painted. Until 1850 there was simply a group of stalls and shacks from which the fish dealers sold their produce. In 1850 the first proper building was put up, and this was painted by Monet in 1871. Three years later this building too had become inadequate; a new building was designed by Sir Horace Jones, architect of the City of London, and opened in 1877.

Boats in the Pool of London

The second painting on a similar theme is still in private hands. Entitled "Boats in the Pool of London", it shows steps and mud-flats below the wharf, and the tall boat, shown upright in the previous picture, has now tilted on its side, awaiting the next tide. The large white bales just might be sugar, as Tate and Lyle's Wharf is nearby.

Notice a well-dressed couple, with the man in a top hat – sitting in one of the rowing boats drawn up at the shoreline. They are about to be ferried across the river, and another such couple is already being rowed, on the left of the painting. One might have thought they could have crossed Tower Bridge, but that Bridge had not yet been built. London Bridge was the lowest bridge across the river until 1894, when Tower Bridge, also designed by Sir Horace Jones, was opened.

One of the few watercolours Turner made of London, uses a viewpoint very similar to that of Monet. Painted probably in 1825, it shows masts of ships where the later Billingsgate would arise. Three spires are visible in this picture. St. Paul's appears like a shadow through the mist, while to its left is the spire of St. Magnus Church. The tallest spire is that of the Monument, 200 feet high, which looms above the Custom House itself. It was erected by Christopher Wren to commemorate the Great Fire of London, and is the tallest isolated stone column in the world. The fact that we can see it shows that Turner was sited considerably further back, towards the South Bank of the Thames, compared with Monet. He was presumably viewing the scene from a boat.

This Turner is full of small figures, including some on the right, who are unloading white bales, similar to those in Monet's picture. Another stands up in the boat, pointing to the Custom House. In the foreground, sailors are lifting a large knotted cable from the river. This probably refers to bonded goods in the Custom House, from which the Customs officers could "lift the bond". Turner liked this sort of pun in his paintings, with a feature inserted into the painting referring to the history of the buildings he was depicting.

J M W Turner: *The Custom House*, 1825.

Vancouver Art Gallery, Canada

Monet: *Boats in the Pool of London*, 1871.

Private Collection

Hyde Park

For his two paintings of London parks, Monet chose Hyde Park and Green Park. Both paintings are rarely seen in England, as they belong to American museums. Hyde Park is the largest of the London parks: it stretches from Green Park up to Oxford Street. It was actually sold off, to three private owners, during the Civil War, but bought back by Charles II. Kensington Palace, which stands in the north-west corner of the Park, was originally a private house. But it was remodelled by Christopher Wren in the 1690's, and then became the principal royal residence for King William and Mary. It remained a royal residence until the reign of George II, but after his death in 1760, Buckingham Palace took over that function. However, several members of the Royal Family still live in apartments there.

The prominent features of the Park are the Serpentine Lake, which was created in the 1730's by damming the Westbourne River, and Rotten Row. This carriageway, running along the Kensington side of the Park, was built by King William III to run between his new Palace at Kensington and his former one at St. James's. Its original name was "route du roi" – French for 'the King's highway' – and during the last century it became the top place for aristocrats and the wealthy to promenade or ride on horseback.

Monet shows, as a path, what is now the main road running from the Serpentine into Bayswater Road, with rows of distinguished houses lining that road, forming the horizon line at the right. They were mainly built in the early 19th century.

Two church spires are visible in the centre and left of the painting. That in the centre is the spire of St. James's, Sussex Gardens. Built in 1843, it soon became the parish church of Paddington. Forty years later, it was enlarged and remodelled by the distinguished architect G E Street. During the last War, a bomb knocked sixty feet off the top of the spire, but the church was lucky to survive: one in twelve houses in the area were completely destroyed. The spire was repaired, as were the stained glass windows, apart from one. Services have continued ever since. To replace the destroyed Baptistery, a new window was created by

A E Buss, and in the lower part of it are shown five scenes or people connected with Paddington. These include the Station, Lord Baden-Powell, founder of the Boy Scouts, an enemy air raid, the statue of Peter Pan in Kensington Gardens, and Sir Alexander Fleming, who discovered penicillin.

The other spire shown by Monet on the far left still exists, but the church has been imaginatively turned into housing. The former Christ Church, Lancaster Gate, can be seen just off the Bayswater Road. Opened in 1855, it lasted until 1978, when it was found to be unsafe. The congregation moved to St. James's and everyone expected Christ Church to be demolished. However, the tower and its graceful spire, the highest in the area, were saved by a scheme which has provided housing as well. An excellent use for a building which would otherwise have disappeared.

Just along Lancaster Gate, west of the former church, is Leinster Gardens. Those who look closely at the terrace of houses here will realise that several are fakes: simply house facades, built over the underground railway which runs underneath. A classic building to surprise your friends with!

Monet has incorporated a dash of red on the skirt of the lady on the left, which complements the green of the grass around it. This technique was often employed by the Impressionists, both the use of complimentary colours, and using a dash of red at some point. They may also have been the first to observe that, the further objects are in the distance, the more blue they appear. (This is caused by their taking on the reflection of the sky.) So, in both his paintings of the Parks, he accurately shows all the distant buildings with a bluish tinge: just the sort of thing official academic artists disapproved of.

Both this and the painting of Green Park show people wandering over the grass of the parks. This must have struck Monet as odd when compared to Paris parks where the public normally walks on the pathways and is often forbidden to walk on the grass. He therefore shows the public walking everywhere except on the pathways: the eccentric English!

Hyde Park, near Bayswater, with Rotten Row in the foreground, 1994

Monet: *Hyde Park*, 1871.

Museum of Art, Rhode Island School of Design Providence, USA

Camille Pissarro: *Rotten Row, Hyde Park*, 1890.

Rotten Row in Hyde Park

Camille Pissarro's 1890 painting of this scene is shown opposite. In the last century, Rotten Row was the major place in which the aristocracy could see and be seen. That may be why Pissarro, with his anti-establishment bias, shows them half hidden behind the trees.

Green Park

Green Park, which spreads between Piccadilly and Buckingham Palace, was first enclosed by King Henry VIII, and then turned into a royal park by King Charles II. He laid out the pathways and built an ice-house beside Piccadilly. This would have been an underground brick chamber, lined with ice, from which one could buy cool drinks. The mound forming the top of this ice-house can still be seen opposite 119 Piccadilly.

For his painting, Monet chose a position near the centre of Green Park, with Piccadilly on his right. He has filled his painting with people strolling around or sitting down: one can even see, on the farther pathway, governesses, or what we now call nannies, wearing white skirts or aprons, and some pushing prams. Monet was looking west towards Apsley House – the town house of the Duke of Wellington. In front of the house stood a massive statue of the Duke on horseback, and that is the tall structure which Monet shows rising above the trees on the left. Constitution Arch now stands in its place, and inside it is a police station: almost the smallest in London. In the centre of the painting are buildings along Piccadilly, some of which were demolished when Park Lane, on the corner of Piccadilly, was widened in the 1950's. Further along Park Lane stood Gloucester House, which was occupied by the Duke of Gloucester and then by the 2nd Earl of Grosvenor. In 1928 this grand building was replaced by the even grander Grosvenor House Hotel. This was the first hotel in London to have a swimming pool, and for five years it also had a skating rink as well. This space was then turned into the Great Room, which in 1943 became an American Officers' Mess. Among those who dined here frequently were Generals Eisenhower and Patton.

Green Park, near Piccadilly, 1994

Monet: *Green Park*, 1871.

Philadelphia Museum of Art

Departure from England

At the end of May 1871, after a stay of some eight months, Monet, his wife and son, boarded a mail-boat. However, they did not return to France. Monet's father had died in January, and he may have wished to postpone paying the necessary death duties. Instead, their boat took them to Rotterdam. From there, they took the train to Amsterdam, and then travelled to the little port of Zaandam, where they stayed till October. In Zaandam, Monet produced a delightful series of paintings of windmills and other buildings beside the water: no less than 25 paintings, but almost all of different scenes. In October they went to Amsterdam, where he produced eleven further paintings, before they returned to France in November 1871.

His friend Pissarro left England in June 1871, and thought it safe enough to return to his home at Louveciennes, in France. It was safe, but he was mortified to find that the occupying Prussians had destroyed over a thousand of his canvases.

The Series Paintings

In the early 1890's, Monet completed three series of paintings: the first of Haystacks, the second of Poplars on the river, and the third, of Rouen Cathedral. But now, instead of using different viewpoints for each painting, he would use one or two viewpoints only, but show those same views as the weather conditions changed. In particular, he loved the way in which fog appeared almost to dissolve the solidity of what he was painting. His first efforts in this field seem to have been his 1870's paintings of the Gare St Lazare in Paris, where he portrayed steam from the trains filling the station.

Later visits to England

Monet took several trips to England in the 1880's, in particular, to stay with his friend, the American painter James Whistler. In 1887 he stayed with him for twelve days, in a studio in the Fulham Road. He must have seen there some of the misty views of the Thames at night in which Whistler specialized.

Pissarro and the Thames

Monet's fellow-Impressionist Camille Pissarro painted the Thames three times: one showing Chelsea Bridge; the others were two versions of the same view, looking from Waterloo Bridge across towards Charing Cross Railway Bridge and the Houses of Parliament. One version is dated 1891 and was completed back in France: the other version, dated 1890, is now in the National Gallery in Washington, and what it shows is very useful in orientating ourselves for the late series by Monet, painted ten years later.

Pissarro was looking towards Charing Cross Railway Bridge, which was built in 1864 and still leads from Waterloo to Charing Cross Stations. In the centre of the painting is the distinctive tower of Big Ben; to the right of that is Westminster Abbey, further right the distinctive small spires of the National Liberal Club, and on the far right is Cleopatra's Needle. The Savoy Hotel, where Monet was later to stay, is just out of sight to the right.

The National Liberal Club was built in the 1880's, designed by Alfred Waterhouse, who also designed the Natural History Museum in Kensington.

Cleopatra's Needle was given to Britain by Egypt in 1819, and brought over from Alexandria in 1878. When erected here, various documents were placed underneath it: the usual coins and memorabilia, but also photographs of twelve of the best-looking women of the day.

Pissarro's painting caused him some difficulty: trying to complete it back in France, he wrote to his cousin Esther Isaacson, asking for a drawing and exact information about the shape of the bridge and its supports. The completed painting was bought by the picture dealer Theo van Gogh, who was Vincent van Gogh's brother.

It was one of at least seven paintings, mainly of central London, produced by Pissarro when he visited England in 1890. He came back twice more: in 1892, when he painted views around Kew Gardens and Green, and in 1897, when he painted views around Chiswick. For details of these, see the author's "Pissarro in West London".

Charing Cross Bridge seen from Waterloo Bridge, 1994

Camille Pissarro: *Charing Cross Bridge*, 1890. National Gallery of Art, Washington, USA

Whistler and The Savoy Hotel

Monet's friend Whistler was also a friend of Richard D'Oyly Carte, the man who had made his fortune by promoting the musicals of Gilbert and Sullivan, and then built the Savoy with the proceeds. It opened in 1889 with César Ritz as General Manager and Escoffier as its chef.

In 1896, Whistler and his wife stayed at the Savoy, in a corner room on the sixth floor. From the balcony of the room, Whistler sketched a view looking towards Westminster, and another looking towards Waterloo Bridge. Just over three years later, Monet started his great series of precisely these two views.

Monet's late London series

Monet came here for the winters of 1899, 1900 and 1901. His three visits produced a total of 94 paintings. They number 34 of Charing Cross Bridge, 41 of Waterloo Bridge and 19 of the Houses of Parliament. For these series, Monet chose to concentrate on one or two scenes seen through different light and weather conditions, as with his series of Rouen. The first two series were seen from his rooms at the Savoy Hotel: the last series was painted across the river from Parliament.

His room at the Savoy now looks straight across at the Royal Festival Hall. Monet wanted to see different effects from the sun shining on the river, so he looked to his left, downstream, towards Waterloo Bridge during the morning, when the sun was in the east. In the afternoon he looked to his right, upstream, towards Charing Cross Railway Bridge, when the sun was coming from the south-west. In the evening, he found the sun setting in the west, behind the buildings of Parliament, and again shining on the river in front of him.

When Monet was here, he saw a very industrial scene. Opposite him across the river (see picture) stood the Lion Brewery, with its proud lion on top, made of Coade stone, a particularly hard-wearing form of artificial stone.

When the brewery was demolished, to make way for the Royal Festival Hall, the lion was removed, and now stands next to Westminster Bridge.

The view across the river in the 19th century: Waterloo Bridge on the left

Charing Cross Bridge seen from the Savoy Hotel, 1994

Monet: *Charing Cross Bridge*, 1899.

Baltimore Museum of Art

Charing Cross Bridge

In his first year, 1899, Monet stayed in the same room that Whistler had occupied. He may have recommended it to Monet.

During that year Monet was accompanied by Alice Hoschedé, who was to become his second wife. (His first wife Camille had died in 1879 aged just 32, leaving two sons behind. Monet was a close friend of Alice and her six children: he and Alice eventually married in 1892, after the death of her first husband.) In London, while Monet painted during the day, Alice and her daughter Germaine went sightseeing with Monet's son Michel, who was already living in England. In 1899, Monet concentrated on the views of Charing Cross Bridge, with Parliament visible beyond.

Cleopatra's Needle is the most prominent object visible from the window now, and it was there in Monet's time. In fact, he included it in two of his earlier sketches (see page 43), but then omitted it from the remaining paintings. He may have decided it broke up the picture too much, by splitting it in two.

The most prominent bridge in this view is Charing Cross Railway Bridge, and in several of the paintings, one can see smoke rising from the steam trains crossing. Beyond, on the right, are the buildings of Westminster, with the tower of Big Ben prominent in front of the Parliament buildings. Big Ben is nowadays the name of the Tower, but actually refers to the largest bell inside the Tower. The clock started operating in 1859, and its chimes are still sometimes broadcast by the BBC at the start of the radio news. Far in the distance, on the left, are the buildings of St. Thomas's Hospital.

The next bridge visible beyond Charing Cross Bridge is Westminster Bridge. This was the first new bridge to be built in London after the medieval London Bridge. Designed and built in stone, it was opened in 1750 and painted several times by Canaletto. The poet Wordsworth wrote a famous poem about it in 1802, which starts, "Earth has not anything to show more fair." It was replaced in 1862 by the present cast-iron bridge, with seven arches, which is seen in Monet's paintings and was designed by Thomas Page.

Canaletto: *Westminster Bridge under construction*, 1746.   Private collection

Waterloo Bridge, seen from the Savoy Hotel, 1994

Monet: *Waterloo Bridge*, 1903.

Waterloo Bridge

Monet also painted the first Waterloo Bridge, designed by John Rennie, and completed in 1817. It was opened by the Prince Regent on the second anniversary of the battle of Waterloo, from which it got its name. The opening of the Bridge is a rare London scene painted by Constable. This bridge was built of granite, with nine arches and two Doric columns decorating the pillars of the arches on each side. It was demolished, despite protests, by the London County Council in 1936, and replaced by the present concrete bridge.

To the right stood the Shot Tower, which in the last century was used to produce lead shot: molten lead was dropped from the top and formed small round balls of shot by the time it reached the bottom. The Tower lasted until about 1962, when it was removed to make way for the concert halls next to the Bridge.

Just the other side of the Bridge stood another shot tower, seen on the left in the engraving reproduced on page 27. It is prominent in several of Monet's paintings of this scene. On its site now stands the National Theatre, and next to it, the tower of London Weekend Television. It was this large industrial area east of Waterloo Bridge, which Monet had as a backdrop to his views of the Bridge. He particularly liked the amount of smoke produced from the chimneys, and complained when they did not produce it.

In particular, on Sundays. "What a dreary day this damned English Sunday is. Nature feels the effects, everything is dead, no trains, no smoke, no boats, nothing to inspire me." That was why he tended to use Sundays to catch up on his correspondence.

An alternative way of painting the same industrial scene is shown in a view from about 1910. Ernest W. Haslehust RBA was an English painter, who illustrated some thirty books in the series "Beautiful England". His painting shows the same part of the riverbank as Monet, with the same shot tower. This time the view is from Waterloo Bridge itself, but Haslehust concentrates on the rusty-colour of the jetties, the barges and their sails, and on all these, and the sky, reflected in the ripples of the Thames. The effect is very striking.

E W Haslehust: *The South Bank from Waterloo Bridge*, circa 1910

The Houses of Parliament seen from across the river, 1994

Monet: *The Houses of Parliament*, 1903.   Brooklyn Museum, New York

The Houses of Parliament

The original Palace of Westminster was built by King Edward the Confessor, whose successor was William the Conqueror. William's son Rufus built Westminster Hall in 1097 AD, and from the 12th century until 1882 it housed the Law Courts. It is now the only medieval part of Westminster to have survived the disastrous fire of 1834, which destroyed the rest of the medieval Palace.

After the fire, nearly 100 architects submitted designs for the new buildings. Charles Barry's Gothic design was selected, and he enlisted the help of Augustus Pugin for the interior decoration. Rebuilding started in 1837, and was completed in ten years.

Monet painted his 19 views of Parliament from St. Thomas's Hospital, which faces Parliament across the river. Slightly confusingly, he omits Big Ben, which is out of his paintings to the right. The tall tower he does show is the Victoria Tower, which is on the southern end of the building, and is the entrance through which the Queen goes to open Parliament each year. The spire he shows is that of St. Stephen's Chapel: under it is the Central Lobby, in which constituents gather in order to 'lobby' their Member of Parliament. Monet went to St. Thomas's in the later afternoon, so his views are even more misty, and often have the sun setting behind the buildings. After visiting the hospital, he wrote, "I saw some superb things there, and can work when and where I want, any day except Sundays."

He mainly worked in the open air, on a roofed terrace of the building nearest the Bridge. Soon after, he wrote to Alice, "If you could see how lovely it is. I wish you had been with me on that terrace: apparently it was cold, and I was so enthusiastic about the work that I didn't notice. I had hardly settled down to paint when the hospital treasurer invited me to come to tea, but he didn't realise I could not leave my painting. I managed to make him understand, not in English, but by gestures indicating how intently I was throwing myself into my work. Ten minutes later the kind man brought me up a cup of tea with sandwiches and cakes: which did me good, actually."

J M W Turner: *Westminster Bridge and the Fire of 1834*.

Philadelphia Museum of Art (see also page 47)

Turner recorded the Fire of Westminster in two oil-paintings, both now in American museums

Leicester Square at night

Also in 1901, Monet started a series of three views of Leicester Square. There are, as it happens, several artistic connections in the Square. The painter Hogarth lived at no 30 from 1733-64, producing some of his best work at that address. A few years later, the American artist John Singleton Copley lived at no 28 from 1776-83. But it is the portrait painter Sir Joshua Reynolds, first President of the Royal Academy in 1768, who has a bust in the square. He lived at no 47 from 1760 until his death in 1792.

Monet's three views were all painted from the first floor of Green's Club, which was situated on the corner of St. Martin's Street, on the south side of the Square. His permission to work there had been arranged by his friend, the American painter John Singer Sargent, who belonged to the Club. Sargent, who lived in England from 1886 onwards, proved a great friend to Monet at this time. He arranged introductions to useful people, and organised a good view from a balcony, when they watched the funeral procession of Queen Victoria in 1901, when Monet stood beside the novelist Henry James. Sargent also took Monet for a walk along the Thames at Chelsea, though sadly, this did not result in any paintings.

The paintings, all in private collections, show the illuminations in the Square at night, and, it is said, the facade of the Empire Theatre. But as the bright colouring of the painting is all on the left of the painting, one wonders if that represents the Palace Theatre, in which case the view is from the west looking eastwards. One of the three paintings was taken up again by the painter in 1918 and partially reworked. Eric Shanes points out that it is very difficult to place white and yellow paint, as seen on the left of this painting, over darker underpainting, without producing a muddy effect. So the brighter colours were added later, presumably in 1918. By that time Monet was producing paintings of waterlilies which were just as impressionistic as these London scenes. With greater experience, he must have felt he knew how to improve on the effects he had tried for in 1901.

Monet: *Leicester Square,* 1901. Private collection

Monet: *Leicester Square,* 1901 and 1918. Private collection

Monet at the Savoy Hotel

To try to deduce where Monet stayed at the Savoy requires considerable detective work. It is known that in 1899 he stayed on the sixth floor, in room 641. This was on the southern corner of the building, and its balcony can be seen in the lithograph view which Whistler produced when he looked out from in the same room in 1896.

In 1900, Monet found that room was not available, as it had been selected by Princess Louise, daughter of Queen Victoria, for convalescing British officers wounded in South Africa in the Boer War. The manager therefore offered him "the corresponding room on the floor below, where the view has a less plunging angle", he complained in a letter to Alice. The next day, he wrote, "I'm well installed on the fifth floor, and have two rooms similar to those we had on the 6th: they took the furniture out of room 541 and I sleep in 542, for with all my equipment I would never have been able to move about."

Unfortunately, since Monet's time all the rooms have been drastically altered and updated, and the balconies used to provide extra room, so that every room could have an ensuite bathroom. The present rooms 641 and 541 are on the other side of the building, but no detailed record has yet been found of the former numbering, to compare it with the present .

Some years ago, the Savoy tried to identify Monet's room by matching the view with the paintings they knew of. Room 508 is currently named as the room concerned, and the modern photos reproduced in this book were taken from that room.

However, the best pointers to Monet's position are the two paintings which show Cleopatra's Needle, and which only came to public attention when one came up for sale at Sotheby's in 1990. As the Needle is halfway between the hotel and Charing Cross Bridge, it gives us a precise reference point. Since he decided to omit the Needle as it destroyed the unity of the picture, one can assume that his two views show it accurately as he saw it, before omitting it from the remaining paintings.

In the painting the Needle appears next to, and on the right of, the second set of pillars from the right of the Bridge. But in the modern photo, taken from room 508, the Needle appears on the left of those pillars (see page 28). Monet's room on the fifth floor was therefore slightly further to the north than the present room 508.

Monet: *Cleopatra's Needle and Charing Cross Bridge*. Private collection

Whistler's two lithographs of the Thames from the Savoy, 1896

The series exhibited

Monet's late London series was only finally revealed to the public in 1904, when he allowed a display of them at his dealer's galleries in Paris. Why so long? In fact, his dealer Durand-Ruel had been pressing him ever since he got back from London in 1901. Theoretically, of course, Monet should have handed over all the paintings once he got back, on the grounds that they must be painted in front of the motif. Instead he held on to them for three years, and continued working on them. When Durand-Ruel complained that he had heard that Monet was even using a photograph, Monet replied, "Whether my paintings were done from nature or not, that is nobody's business and is not important. The result is everything."

Return to England

After the success of the Paris show, Monet returned to Britain six months later, in December 1904, to try to organise a similar exhibition in London. Once again, he stayed at the Savoy. But this time, he wrote to his wife,

"The Savoy has greatly changed and is now far too luxurious, and I find it less pleasant. Impossible to get a room overlooking the river: it's full of people."

He wrote to his dealer from the Savoy: "I have always wanted to show my London paintings here, for my own satisfaction." That never happened in his lifetime, which may help to explain why not one of this late series is in a public collection in London. But one must remember the prices they fetched. After 1904, his paintings of Waterloo and Charing Cross Bridges went for the modern equivalent of £30,000 each, while his nineteen paintings of Westminster went for £40,000 each. Little wonder his annual income at this time was around £425,000. In contrast with Britain, at least twenty-four of this series are now in public collections in America. It is surely about time this anomaly was rectified. At least one of Monet's paintings of Waterloo Bridge, of Charing Cross Bridge, and of Westminster, should be bought and put on permanent display in a public gallery or museum in London. Then we shall finally have done justice to this great series.

Room 508 at the Savoy Hotel, 1994

Monet's last years

Monet moved to his grand house in Giverny in 1883. In later life, he entertained many prominent friends there, including the French Prime Minister Clemenceau, who arranged for his major waterlily paintings to be given to the French nation.

Monet died at Giverny on 6th December 1926, when he was 86. When Clemenceau heard of his death, he hurried down to Giverny, 400 miles from his home, and arrived as the body was being put into the coffin. As the undertaker's men were drawing a black sheet over the body, he tore a flowered curtain from the window and laid it in place instead, saying, "No black for Claude Monet." How right he was!

Turner and the impressionists

Both Monet and Pissarro acknowledged a debt to Turner, though both were circumspect in doing so. Viewing the painting opposite (and comparing also page 39), one can see how Turner could be described as the first of the Impressionists.

Bibliography

The most detailed accounts of Monet's stays in London are to be found in two books: "Monet in London", by Grace Seiberling, published by the High Museum of Art, Atlanta, Georgia, USA, in 1988, and "Claude Monet in Great Britain", by Sylvie Patin, in both English and French, pub. Hazan, Paris, 1994. The former writes intelligently about the composition of the paintings; the later quotes extensively from Monet's correspondence and writes about the many events in London which Monet witnessed and described. Both are thorough and well researched works, though neither book gives any indication that its author had visited London.

For Turner's paintings of the Burning of the Houses of Parliament, see "Dreadful Fire: the Burning of the Houses of Parliament", by K. Solender, Cleveland Museum of Art, 1984.

For an enjoyable detective novel in which the hero tracks down unknown 1871 paintings by Monet and Pissarro, see "The Wrong Impression", by John Malcolm, pub. Collins, 1990.

J M W Turner: *Burning of the Houses of Parliament,* 1834. Cleveland Museum of Art (see also page 39)

Lilburne Press

Lilburne Press specialises in publishing books about art history and local history. Most of its publications feature a painter in a locality, and show local scenes as painted by an artist about a century ago, along with a modern photo of the same scene from the same angle.

Most of its publications are written by Nicholas Reed BA (Oxon), MA (Manc), M.Phil. (St. A).

Among his books are:

Camille Pissarro at Crystal Palace (1987; 3rd ed. 1995)

Pissarro in Essex (1992)

Pissarro in West London (1990; 4th ed. 1997)

Sisley and the Thames (1991; rev. 1992)

Richmond and Kew Green: A Souvenir Guide (1992)

Whose Cat Are You? Forty Celebrities' Cats (1994)

Edith Nesbit in SE London and Kent (1998)

Lilburne Press also publishes *A Guide to Impressionist Paris*, by Patty Lurie (1996). This too has comparative paintings and modern photographs. With 180 pages and 160 colour illustrations, it shows how the various Impressionists: French, English and American, fit into the Impressionist movement.

Nicholas Reed

Nicholas specialises in placing artists in their local context, and is a lecturer for the National Association of Decorative and Fine Arts Societies. His most popular lecture is Artists' Views of the Thames through Five Centuries.

In 1985-7 he was Founder-Chairman of the Friends of Shakespeare's Globe and in 1989-92 was Founder-Chairman of the Friends of West Norwood Cemetery. In 1996 he became Founder-Chairman of the Edith Nesbit Society, and in 1999 he intends to establish an Impressionist Society. Further details from him, c/o Lilburne Press.